sincerely,

F.S. YOUSAF

central
avenue
publishing

2020

Published by Central Avenue Publishing, an imprint of Central Avenue Marketing Ltd.
www.centralavenuepublishing.com

SINCERELY,

Trade Paperback: 978-1-77168-192-6
Epub: 978-1-77168-193-3
Mobi: 978-1-77168-194-0

Published in Canada
Printed in United States of America

1. POETRY / Love   2. POETRY / Asian American

10 9 8 7

THIS BOOK WAS ORIGINALLY MEANT
FOR ONE SPECIAL PERSON IN MY LIFE.
NOW, THOUGH, IT IS MEANT FOR ALL
THE SPECIAL PEOPLE. THOSE WHO LIGHT
UP YOUR DAY WITH THE SIMPLICITY OF
THEIR SMILE.

THIS IS FOR THEM.

July 27th, 2018. 12:36 p.m.

We sat at a local diner; you drove all the way here just to be with me. You must have known what would happen, but you hid your excitement behind talking about the past, present and future. We talked about all the things we usually did, like what we would do once we got married, once we could be with one another for this life, and eventually the next. You would gently touch my hand, then take my home fries, and ask me to finish your pancakes. It was a day just like any other, but we both knew it would be different.

Lunch finished, we drove to the gazebo where you had once trekked two hours to see me when my life seemed a mess. A seemingly long time passed before we could say anything. We were commenting on the slightly brisk breeze, and the wonder of it on this sunny July day. You rested your arm on my left pocket, attempting to feel some sort of box (which you later admitted), but I had the ring stashed in my back pocket, and this book under my shirt. And we began talking about the kind of life we both wanted to lead, and how that might look for us.

I wanted this moment to be private. I didn't want a flash of a camera, or snapshot of what our life would look like, both of us standing together, fighting every battle, celebrating every win. And so I took this book out, its cover with the night sky intended to reflect the location of the constellations on the day we met. I watched you read. And read. And read. Until you got to "An Ode to You." When you finished it, tears were streaming down your cheeks, and you looked up. I was in front of you, on one knee, with the ring in my hand. Asking for you to marry me.

Asking for you to spend eternity with me.

Asking you to be mine.

Asking you to take me as yours . . .

You pushed me to get this book out to the world. Its success is owed to you, and to God for having had us meet.

So here it is, dear readers. This is an ode to her and to you. An ode to everyone you love, and have loved. Think of them as you read this, because surely, I was thinking of one as I was writing these poems.

Sincerely,

F.S. Yousaf

STABILITY

Our story began with strength,
A foundation built over time.
Cemented over with trust
And fruitful commitment.
A base which would not crumble
Or crack under the stress
Of what was built on top of it.

DILEMMA

I am struggling between
The thoughts of destiny
And what stands before me.

My heart is torn between the two,
And even though I do not know
What the future holds,
I hope the path I take
Has been written in stone.

HESITATE

I refuse to store
All my joy in you.
For if you ever leave,
I would not know what to do.

ENCHANT

Waiting for the past
Was no longer an option.
Placed in my view
Was a woman
Who had captivated me.

PAST-TIME

Loveless lies / Lustful eyes.
That was all I knew
Until you appeared before me.

And I would be lying to you
If I told you I do not still think
Of that time before,
But only to compare it to my happiness now,
And how I wish I had found you sooner.

MIGRATE

I remember you told me
That birds gave you hope.
I understand now
That you could not bear to stay
In the same place for too long.

BELIEF

How do you suppose
You can capture
Your true potential
When you speak
As if your aspirations
Are hopeless?

DEPTH

I did not just fall in love
With your beauty,
I fell in love with every single
Aspect of you.
And I pray that everybody else
Can see what I see in you.

FLOAT

Do not bury me
Deep within your mind,
For it is already filled
With chaos and pain.
Let me be
One of the good thoughts
On the surface.

PACIFY

I have fallen furiously in love with you.
So hell-bent and damned
To call you my own,
That my heart burns
At not being able to fully capture
The soothing aura you give off.

FORMER STORIES /
BETTER CONCLUSIONS

You were the girl
I wanted to charm with my writing,
For I knew that average words would not work
With you.
You were remarkable,
And craved the spontaneous kind of love
That ill-fated writers had,
The ones that only reside
In history books and novels.

I pray our story does not end like theirs.
I only desire a tale of stability and peaceful mornings.

WHERE THE HEART IS

I have jumped from house to house
My whole life.
Stability, for me, has been nearly nonexistent,
But I have hope
That you could be my home
For as long as I live.

GENESIS

Have you ever considered
The way your name
Rolls off my tongue?

Have you ever witnessed
A soul in another?
Or did you recognize mine
The very first time I spoke to you?

I hope your search has ended with me.
I pray we begin our journey together.

AFTERLIFE

How the world feels
When I am with you
Can only be seen as a preview
Of the boundless peace
And unrelenting happiness
That only lies
In the hereafter.

FANTASY

I have thought of you
Every night / every morning.
And in-between
I find meaning—
Hidden in stories
Which we can only imagine,
Hidden in the adventures
Which we can only dream.

ANTICIPATION

Keep on talking about how lovely
Our future will be.
As every word escapes your mouth,
Glimpses of hope
Appear in my heart.

WHAT IS YOURS IS MINE

I did not enter your life
To hold you back from your goals—
To make you feel miniscule.
I crave success for you,
Even more so than for myself.

CONFIDANT

I stared into your eyes,
Got lost in what you are,
And found myself unable to focus elsewhere.
You clearly knew my weakness.

PROCESS

I desired the world for her,
But I could not afford it.
She was content with
The little I could do,
As long as I strived
For not only what was best for me,
But for the two of us.

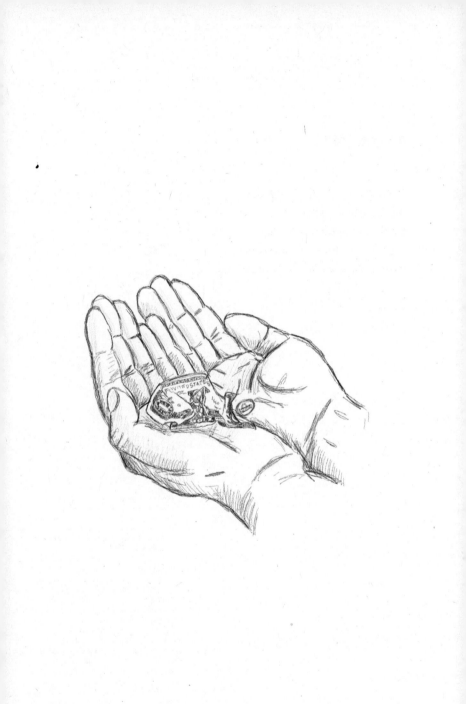

PRESENT

I ended up loving the moment
More than the memories.
I would rather be with you,
And see you blossom day by day,
Than remember how we used to be.

FULFILLMENT

I cannot recall
A stressful silence
Taking over for our words.
She was thrilled to see me,
As I was in awe of her.

And together
We both felt utterly complete.

CAROUSEL

When I want to write about bliss,
I think of you.
When I want to write about tranquility,
I think of you.
When I want to write about the beauty of this world,
My mind wanders only towards you.

UPWARD

My life before you was
Before spring flowers blossomed.
Before the skies remained clear and blue.
Before a smile would remain
In my heart.

My life after meeting you
Is a new chapter I gladly bask in.
Taking in all the good
For I had not experienced anything like it before.

My life after meeting you
Is a chapter I hope I never forget.

DÉJÀ VU

I asked you how our love was doing,
And you responded by saying
That it was as tight as a knot.

And while your words gave me déjà vu,
I turned back and asked you again
After some time,
How is our knot doing now?

And you responded,

Tighter than before.

AFFABLE

You have so much love
For the people you surround yourself with
That I question the very possibility of it.

And uniquely enough,
I find your love growing
Even more
With each new soul
You encounter.

You pick your flowers in handfuls,
Without giving a thought
To the stems that land
Between the creases of your palms.
You make sure of their crisp petals,
And stern stem,
Hoping they will last you a lifetime.

HUE

I loved the scenes
You could paint with your stories.
You finally put some
Color in my mind.

AWAIT

I always counted down the days
Until I saw you again.
These moments with you
Were the only times
I felt like my true self.

ONE OF A KIND

I have not witnessed
The kind of grace that you carry
Within anyone else.
Consider it a rare specialty.

RECALL

The bond we share
Is exquisitely genuine
And undoubtedly natural;
Our souls may have met
In a past time.

LOVESICK

I imagine more than
What is good for me,
But that is only because
I am stuck daydreaming
Over what we may do next.

RELEASE

Having to admit
That you had become
An important part of me
Was a liberating,
Yet terrifying moment.

I would redo it all the same.

VOYAGE

Take me to the places
Which I have never seen,
And tell me the stories
Of their past.

Teach me the many ways to live,
More than I have ever known.

PERSEVERE

Life tends to throw
Stones at you,
But your kindness and strength
Somehow turn those stones
Into words of perseverance
For people who need it most.

LETTERS TO

One of my many goals in life
Is to give you the type of love
That I had always desired.

UNCLOUDED

When I meet your gaze,
I see that you are staring at me—
Not my figure, or size.
But you are staring at me as if
I am made of glass,
Witnessing all that I am made of.
Knowing my innermost workings,
And which way the tide turns
Within me.

You gaze upon me
With truthful eyes,
Seeing who I truly am
And what I have a chance
To become,
Instead of what others may whisper
Behind backs and closed doors.

AMAZE

There is something so sweet
About the way your voice sounds
Early in the morning.
It reminds me of a time
When I believed that happiness
Was unreachable.
But I am here,
Astonished by the way
You make me feel.

RENEWAL

I was told
That the feelings would die down.
But here I am,
Excited for every new day
I get to spend with you.

OUR DAYS

Your scent lingers on me
Long after you have departed.
It tells me the story
Of our day spent together,
And I enjoy thinking back to it,
Since it will be yet another distant memory
Come tomorrow.

My mind carries your distinct fragrance,
A humble reminder that I am
Nowhere near you at the moment.

VIBRANCE

Falling autumn leaves
Remind me of you.
You made the descent look beautiful,
And brought color
To the very ground you fell on.

UNSATISFIED

How could I possibly be content
With an outcome
That is everything
But you and me?

VISION

Once we harmonized,
Your goals and dreams
Also became mine.
And I so dearly
Wanted to see you
Achieve them all.

SENSE

You knew it was a lie,
Even when I pleaded
"I'm fine, I promise."
You could tell
By the way
Anxiety danced in my eyes.

And I am forever grateful
That you know every inch of me.

HOOKED

The first thing I fell in love with
Was the way you wrote,
So sweet,
So innocent,
Light on my mind
And had me high
All the time.

SOWN

You came into my life
To show me
That mere moments
Can create lasting memories.
You revived my hopeless eyes,
So I could see
The true beauty
The world held.

JOURNAL ENTRY: ONE YEAR LATER

You enlightened my mind and softened my heart. Your laugh was the kind that brightened up a gloomy day. You were caring, and I envied that you beat my love for you tenfold. You were exactly what people looked for, and just what I needed.

NEWFOUND LOVE

The laughs we share are new,
But the bond we share is old,
Reminiscing almost-forgotten moments.
And while we were lost for some time,
Perhaps wandering through the endless corridors,
And mistakenly taking wrong turns,
I am glad we have found one another again.

LOVE

You became the occupant of my mind,
The beat of my heart,
And the tranquility in my soul.
You became my life,
My solace,
The best person I ever knew.

OUR STORY

While I sit here
In the midst of the night,
Writing away to you,
I think of every single little
Memory that makes us whole.
The good, and even the bad.
They have led us to
Each other's sanctuary.

DIFFERENCE

A better life
Was one of the many
Things you offered me,
And they were the most refreshing words
I had ever heard.

ACCEPTANCE

I felt your presence
Even in my most lonesome moments.
What an opportune time
To recognize your love.

JOURNAL ENTRY: MEMORIES

We sat over steaming cups of coffee, in the aroma-filled cafe.
You took a cappuccino, but they forgot the almond milk you
requested. You wore a grey coat, with a cozy scarf around your
neck. The sunglasses complemented your ensemble perfectly.
My eyes softened with every look at you. You said we would sit
for a short while, but we sat for an hour, maybe even two. Talking
about our life, and what we could do. I enjoyed the moment so
completely, and your smile had me at a peace, the smile you'd
shelve away here and there. The time went by quickly, and you
had to leave. I wished we could have sat for longer, echoing our
lives and desires.

EYE OPENING

How alive you were
When all else was withering.
How valiantly you stood
When so much around you was falling apart.

Your strength was inspirational—
And your drive, immeasurable.
So much I had not seen
Until you came to me,
And I can say with confidence
That I would not have it any other way.

HOLD ON JUST A LITTLE LONGER

Search for me in my silence
And search for me
When my rambunctious nature
Takes over the calm and peace.
Search for me,
For I do not search for myself.
Aid in finding me
For I may never find myself on my own.

– I will find my own voice soon

YEARN

Hold me until my breathing calms,
When my heart is not pounding
Through my chest with a rib-shattering ferocity.
Hold me even after the exhausted slumber
That comes with these cursed episodes.
And as much as I wish for them
To leave me be,
Your presence comforts my mania
With unbounding hope for an uncomplicated future.

ASSISTANCE

I ask myself constantly:

What if there is no cure for this ache,
This pain that resides in me?

And although you cannot fix the ache
You are there to help me through the journey
So I do not wander this dark path alone.

OUTREACH

You bring me happiness,
But you are not the cure
For my sadness.
That I must find
On my own.

HOMEBOUND

Every breath I shared with you
Felt as if I was reborn.
A clean slate
And a vast amount of time
To improve upon my imperfections.

With you,
I was accepted with open arms.

SOLACE

I often remember days
When sadness had confiscated my mind.
Being a man with barely
A sense of direction,
I considered myself hopeless.

Instead of being alone
I am in your arms now,
Traveling to serenity.

SAVIOR

You saved me
From the dangers of my mind—
Your hand
Was the only one
That could reach me.

ENDEAVOR

I acknowledge that

I may be a negative person,
But when someone hurls negativity at me,
I do my utmost to be positive.

I do it for reasons unknown to me.

I acknowledge that negativity may barge through
Barriers and anchor us down,
And when that happens I intend to be positive
For both our sakes.
I may fail, but I will try and try again
Until I get it just right.

We've got whatever comes our way.

MOTIVE

I may throw my hands up
In defeat,
But you always seem
To catch my wrists before
They leave my side.

Your eyes beg me to persevere.
For who knows,
Success and happiness
May be closer than they seem.

BUOYANT

There is a deep fog in my mind,
One which surrounds me every day
As I take aimless steps towards escaping.

Even when I think of you
The fog does not dissipate.
My body remains the same:
Trapped in a boundless cloud.

But what the thought of you does
Is give me some sense of direction—
A purpose for me to keep pushing forward
And never give up.
No matter the days that have passed
Or how many steps I may have to retrace.

For who knows,
Perhaps one day
I may be able to see the sky again.

REBORN

Three years ago
I had difficulty thinking of the future.
I could not think past
The minutes and hours
That lay ahead of me.
I was living day by day,
Anticipating some
Sort of end.

Your timely arrival
Was a memorable one.
And I thought to myself
That this could possibly be
The person who can surely
Ignite a fire in me.

You saved me
From myself,
And make every day
Worth looking forward to.

CARETAKER

I asked if the ill feelings
That lodged themselves between
The slim openings of my ribs were
Normal to feel,
And you disagreed with me
With every ounce of air
That could fill your lungs.

Show so much grace in your actions
That others cannot tell
You harbor any ill feeling within.

You helped in unleashing
The best parts of me
And aided in combatting my faults
Instead of discarding them.

Oh, the way you cherished my heart.

MY ANTIDOTE

I do not love you
Just for the sake of loving,
But because you have given me
Tranquility on days
Where I have given up on myself.

FOREVER IN MY MIND

The lullabies you sing
Are soul-soothing
To the point where they have
Become a part of my healing from
My ill-fated thoughts.

LIFELINE

With you being the only certainty in my life,
I decided to abandon the fear
Of losing you.
Knowing that our time here is temporary
But acknowledging the love
We share will live on for eternity.

NOOR

Your fondness for me outshines
The others in my life—
My eyes have just not
Adjusted to your light.

CARRY

You found my drunken, hopeless body
In the middle of the night,
And while the rest left nature
To deal with my remains,
You took me into your care
And nurtured me to strength.

Behind every great man there is a greater woman.

Behind me there was you.

GUARD

There have been moments
Where you saw me hurting–
Ever since the beginning
When the dark clouds would hover over me,
You would not run away,

But run towards the storm,
Providing shelter
To a person so comfortable
With having no one there before.

THE WORLD AWAITS US

I am aware
That you look at everyone else,
Aching to do
The things we cannot.
I promise that in time
We will reach those points.

EXISTENCE

Small moments of comfort
Were the ones
When you stood in front of me,
Smiling like no tomorrow.
When your eyes became lost in mine,
And my eyes
Became lost in you.

REAFFIRMATION

I have loved you for years,
Which in turn have felt like
An entire lifetime.
Our vows renew
When we are nearly broken,
And we keep the love
Ever flowing.

83

EVERLASTING

There is so much life in you
That I tend to feel exhausted
From the constant upkeep.
But the exhaustion that strikes
Is one I look forward to—
It makes me feel undoubtedly alive
And leaves me wishing for the days
To last for as long
As you are with me.

ZAKAT

The happiness which surrounds you is immeasurable,
And instead of hoarding it all,
You donate it with a smile
Paired with your calm demeanor.
A gracious contribution
To those who felt
As if all were lost.

JANNAH

We promised each other forever,
And I find myself praying for that vow
To be fulfilled under a celestial date tree
Which stretches farther than our eyes can see,
And by rivers freely flowing
With milk and honey.

I pray our love is heavenly
Enough to be suited
For the hereafter.

PRAYERS

Please give her strength,
For my efforts are minimal
Compared to her adversity.
Make her stronger for herself,
And give me another reason
To look up to her.

D U A

The sky is weeping
And the ground
Is filling up with angels' tears.
Today all I'm praying for
Is you.

ARTIST

I am captivated
By God's art.
Every sunrise,
Sunset,

And you.

SABR

Many stand in our way,
Refusing to let us live
The life we have always envisioned.
But as long as we have resilience
And faith,
We will never be stopped.

RESILIENT

One of the very qualities
I admired about you
Was your bond with God,
How it stood, unwavering,
Even in the fiercest of storms.

How no matter what happened,
Your faith did not falter,
And you accepted that
You were never alone.

FLOURISH

The love I cherish most
Is in the form
Of an eternal flame.
Through wind and storm,
Rising, and never dwindling.

CURE

You have many sleepless nights,
And it pains me to know
That you are not getting the rest
You desperately need.
I will be there soon,
And hopefully my presence helps.

INFORMAL

I was told that before
Our souls are exhaled into our bodies
We meet one another in a place which we cannot remember
Any longer.

When I met you,
It was as if there was already
An established comfort and familiarity
Between us.
As if we had known each other
For many, many years.

GROUNDED

I have stood by you
In glory
And in pain.
What makes you think
That I am not here
To stay?

MONUMENT

Of all the places
Where we have traveled,
Your happiness
Has been my favorite sight.

DAYDREAMING

I seem to be calm,
Smiling larger
And laughing with ease.
My thoughts do not disturb me,
As they are too busy
Orbiting around you.

REKINDLE

It is said
That some people are meant for one another.
That the ones who mingle in this life
Are the ones who met in heaven before
Their lives began.

That connection—
A familiar lightning
That struck as soon
As we spoke our first words
To one another.

I had heard you before
In a place where we are no more,
And I am delighted
That our souls have been reunited once again.

FORTITUDE

Your heart has so much room for love
That I sit here,
In complete wonder
At how it could possibly be so.

You have seen
And felt terrible emotions—
Some which made you feel
Minuscule and beneath the ground.

I am here for you
Through the storms and the calm.
I am here for you
Through the anger
And the peace.
I am here for you
Through the frustration,
And tranquility.

You do not deserve most
Of the fires that come your way,
Yet you handle them gracefully.
As if you have lived with them
Lifetimes over.

It pains me how little
I can do,
But I hope the sincere amount I give
Brings you a degree of happiness.

DEFINING LOVE

Your soft lips tease me
As I am lying in bed,
Watching you dream up storms.

The first time I spoke to you,
I did not know that we would be here,
Falling for one another
The way we have.

Many moons have set,
And many suns have risen.
I ask myself why,
Through all my chaotic emotions,
You have been constant.

It's not that I fell for you,
Or planned for this story;
It all happened in a whirlwind.
Even past our first words shared,
You found comfort within me
As I did with you.

Comfort within a person.
That's what our love is.

TEND

Barren land that cannot grow life.
My bond with you—
Soft dirt which has been fertilized tenderly.
Seasons blessing us greatly,
Nurturing a growth
That is soon to come.

HAVEN

We carve our initials on trees,
Hoping for others to see—
To be a reminder of
How our love has grown.
Wild, untamable,
And thick like the trunk
Of the old tree.

A reminder that our love
Is a shelter for us,
Providing shade
For whatever weather may come our way.

REBORN

I lend you my time
In trying to set you free.
Helping your revival—
Watching you flower
Into what you always dreamed to be.

KILN

Out of the ash from the fire we made
Comes out stronger chains,
Something we forged together from
The heat we created.
Gaining more strength in our love
Than we ever had on our own.

WAVELENGTH

We move at the same time,
Limb by limb,
And make sure that both of us
Are on the same page before
Moving even further.

ENTHRALL

Her voice
Could capture me easily.
Like a riptide
Sweeping me against my will.
The sheer strength and power
Was mesmerizing
On its own.

IMMERSED

Our letters of love
Became the bridge
To deeper understanding.
A place where ordinary words
Could not survive.

RECALL

When our paths crossed,
I felt as if we had met
In another time.
Your laugh had me in thought,
Your smile had me dreaming,
And your joy
Left me in awe.

UNFAMILIAR

I am so entirely filled with love
That I feel guilt
In not being able to share these
Emotions with others.

As if I am finally being watered
After years of being barren,
All while knowing others do not feel
The sweet liberation of compassion.

I will never get used to this splendor.

HIGH NOON

You may be afraid to love fully
Because of how temporary this life is,
So let's make memories
That will flourish within us
No matter how long
Or short we live.

ATTAIN

The love would flow in the air,
Finding its way to everyone besides myself.
And while there was a clear lack of love in my heart,
I found that drowning my sorrows
In medication and temporary passion
Appeased my longing for what would never arrive.

And yet, I was wrong.

I became even more fulfilled than I could ever imagine
When God sent a love that would never dwindle
Throughout time.

LETTERS TO

I always told myself
That I could not possibly
Fall more in love with you.
But here you are,
Proving me wrong once again.

GRASP

Holding your hand
Was an art that even
I could not understand.
But I would have given all the time
I had to master it.

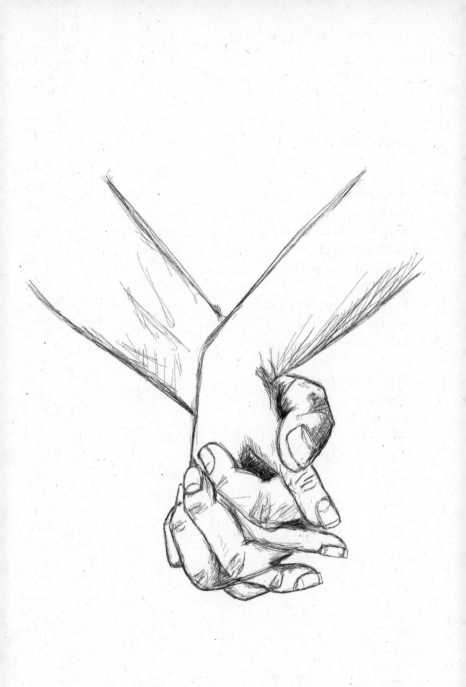

COMPROMISE

When you crumble,
I hurt with you.
But I do not stand idly by.
I will extend my hands
And catch every piece
As you fall.
I will be by your side as you
Rebuild, and help you
In the process.

You are half of me,
A purer, gentler half.
I am not whole when you
Are not whole yourself.

STAMINA

There have been numerous fights,
Some which have left us torn
And thinking of our end.
But love is not love
Without trials that test endurance.
What would we be if we were to quit
At the worst of moments?

RECOURSE

There are speckles of art
And humanity stuck within you, my dear.
You are the one
Who can choose to unleash
Or imprison them.

ALTER

We sacrificed plenty
To make sure
Our future
Did not suffer
The same fate
As our past.

SOFTHEARTED

Give the good a place in your heart,
No matter if it is the size of
A speck of dust.
Nurture it, care for its needs.
Watch it become new
Until it consumes you whole.
And when it does,
Sit back
And let its beauty envelop you.

TRIALS

While the love we carry
Has given us peace,
It has brought along hardship as well.
A hardship that would test us—
Enough to cause distress,
But not more than we could take.

A test which would cause pain,
But also bring clarity
To the way we were meant for one another.

BEAM

The light may not enter today
Or tomorrow,
But throughout time
Young rays will begin to peek
Into the darkness of your heart,
And your heart will soften
With the warmth that comes with.

WANDERER

I have seen you travel this world,
Basking under the Parthenon,
Walking the streets of Pompeii,
Admiring the beauty of the Hagia Sophia

While you were without me during this time,
I only aspire to see them with you,
So I can experience this world
With no one else.

DISTANCE

The distance was unusual,
And the separation—cruel.
But real love never fades,
And I will ultimately
Be by your side.

BOUNDLESS

Our road may be a bit jagged
And sporadically smooth.
The bumps come as they please.
Seemingly created from the air we breathe.

We are defined as works-in-progress
And will be so our entire lives.
As long as we do not stop in the tracks,
What we have can flourish
And be built further
Than the eye can see.

ACKNOWLEDGE

I would be a fool to compare
Your presence to that
Of a candle burning valiantly in a dark room,
Acting as a guide as some would say.
For you would eventually burn out,
Leaving me alone with no sense of direction.

You are closer to a star
On an unpolluted night,
Your light making its way to me
No matter the distance.
And even though you are
Hidden at times,
Knowing you are always there
Brings me a sense of relief.

UNITED

I came closer
As you distanced yourself.
I will not let you
Fight alone.

STUPOR

The way you spoke
Had me from
The very first word,
To the silence
That followed.

EXEMPLAR

These trials.
The difficulty you feel
Does not go unnoticed.

You are a warrior in my eyes,
One who stands tall,
Pushing back against adversity.
Your shadow casting larger
Than you believe it to be.

To witness your strength is extraordinary,
Inspiring,
And everything
Which gives me the desire
To have that same power
You carry.

ROOTS

You have come a long way
Since your journey began,
So much so
That you have forgotten
How you used to be.

Do not forget those times,
When you believed the world to be
Larger than you could ever imagine.
For if you do
You are likely to repeat
Your history once again.

RUSH

There have been so many memories
Made between the two of us.
The majority irreplaceable
And all of them unforgettable.
As if I am holding some sort
Of pleasant grudge that I will always clutch.
Knowing those very feelings will
Unfailingly tackle my body
At the very sight of you.

SUNDAY MORNING

I would rather be resting
In your arms,
Beneath the comfort
Of a sun-laden blanket.
Where the scent of rain
Has freshened the earth.

WORLD OF OUR OWN

I want to live to see
The world in action,
And traveling with anyone
That is not you
Would not bring me
The same satisfaction.

RECOLLECTION

There are moments
Where I look at you and wonder;

An emotion of younger times
Rushes to my mind.
One which I have not felt
In many years.
And yet you still trigger this sense
Of nostalgia
Which keeps my head in the clouds
And body present
In the midst of the flurry.

Those years—
Stress does not plague
My joints or mind;
Sadness does not hold even
An ounce of my being hostage.

And this euphoria,
This peace eventually dwindles,
But seems to arrive
When I am in need of it most.

FLASHES OF DELIGHT

When I think of you
All that comes to mind
Is the laughter and delight.
Lighthearted memories and joyous emotions
That I tend to not feel occasionally.
And with those thoughts
Comes an overbearing longing
To be around you once again.

SEPTEMBER 7, 2015

Skipping over the bridge,
Hands wide out,
Grey cardigan waving in the wind
While I smiled behind you.

Here I see someone,
Someone I had been patient with
For a long time.
Not bad-patient,
But good-patient.

I saw our love blossom,
Like a rose in spring.
Firm, strong, and beautiful.
My heart beat for you
Every second, every day.

You leaned on me,
And we talked about our days
And what else we could accomplish.
I felt your heart sync with mine
And I never wanted to let go.

Twirling, hands in the air,
Dancing in the cool summer's breeze.
Walking, talking, standing real close.
I prayed this was something
That would get stronger
As time passed.

FLORESCENCE

My love is a yellow sunflower,
So vibrant
One may mistake it for the sun
When they look at it from afar.

A flower which blooms no matter
The sky that stands above it—
One which does not bend
In mighty gusts.

But with its strength and vibrance,
There comes a day it will be snipped,
Possibly by a man hoping
To gain a toothy smile from his muse.

One leaf and a half-stem and roots still
Planted stubbornly in the
Soft soil below—
It will grow to its former self.

No matter the time it takes,
No matter what comes its way.
The flower will bloom once more.

BLISS

Like the animals
That scurry across prairies—

Shimmering grass
In the slight breeze.

A child who bolts across concrete,
In blissful ignorance
Of what the harm of falling
Will do to their body.

A love so fierce
That no fire can be called upon
To be compared to it.
Surely, it will grow insecure
Of its adversary.

And like the animals
That scurry,
And the grasses that shimmer,
And the child who runs,
We are filled with carefree
Tendencies,
While strips of sunlight reach us gently.
And the breeze caresses us.

And a love so strong
That when I gaze towards you,
I do not question where we stand—
For I know the answer
Just by the way you smile at me.

EVERYTHING I SAW IN YOU

You asked me why I loved you, and why I didn't want to move on.
So I had to list everything.

It was your smile, the one that I always asked for. That
contagious smile that made my heart pound even faster than it
already was when I was with you.
It was how wide your eyes got when they saw me or anything else
that you loved.
It was your face: the way you would squint when you broke into
laughter.
It was your laughter that was, indeed, music to my ears. (A new
song at midnight.)

You were a book of quotes—one of the largest I had seen.
Hemingway, Plath, Poe—I could fill bookcases with all who
influenced you.

It was how you'd cry at TV shows, hoping for a happy ending.
It was the sass when you weren't getting your way.
It was your stubbornness when you were set on an idea, only to
soften throughout time and with some thought.
It was the way you never gave up, even when the outcome looked
bleak.

You were enticing, beautiful, breathtaking; I kept on finding a new way to compliment you every time I had a chance to study you.

You understood me even though you never experienced my difficulties. You were sad when I was, and I cried when you did.

We were a team, something we'd never been before.

I didn't just fall in love with your beauty, I fell in love with every single little aspect of you. And I pray that everybody else can see what I saw in you.

EUPHORIC

Resting under the lightly colored sheets,
As we whisper purely
Into each other's ears.
Holding on as if our lives
Depended on it,
Cherishing the moment
So our dreams would not wither
Like flowers in autumn.

Skin so tender,
Air so sweet.
Door closed,
The windows dare not speak.
These feelings cannot escape,
And will stay in our midst for as long
As we allow them to live.

VIRTUAL HISTORY

Would we have met
In the streets
Of our motherland?

Possibly over a cup of steaming chai,
Standing next to the street vendor
Around the corner.
The smell of tainted air
And the buzzing of motorcycles surrounding us.

Or would we become lost
In the crowds of similar faces and dress?

I was made for you,
As you were for me.
In this life
And every life there possibly
Could be.

For who knows?
I might catch your glance in a passing moment,
As we are divided by the sea of vehicles filling the narrow street.
Or we might bump in the midst
Of the ocean of bodies.
Creating the same story
We are creating

Now.

AN ODE TO YOU

When I first saw you
I could hardly pull my eyes from you,
Leaving me full of unfamiliar emotion,
Leaving me breathless.

You left me wondering,
Over a hot cup of coffee,
Under the beaming sun outside my favorite café.

Maybe you could be the person I'd spent my life looking for,
And carried the power to change my life for the better. I
Rolled the dice once, I
Rolled the dice twice, and yet,
You refused to leave my mind.

Maybe you could be good for me;
Even destiny could be pointing towards your name.

(Now read every single letter at the beginning of each
sentence...)

will you
marry me?

SEPTEMBER 2ND, 2018

I haven't written a vow before—I hope that isn't surprising.
So, forgive me.
I may not do as well as you expect.

When our paths first intertwined,
Mine was packed with obstacles—
I was one who found life difficult.
I was one who constantly chased after familiarity.

And I craved negativity, for that's all I ever knew and saw
in my young life.
So, if you cannot tell,
Your arrival was shocking,
But also, simply lovely.
It was something I needed, but could not
See it at that time.

Deciding to marry you was one
Of the easier choices in my life.
There's just this quality about you
That brings comfort to my whole being.

And while our journey together
Over the past couple years has been
Filled with mountains and simple landscapes,
I'm glad that there have been countless moments
Where our love unearthed itself
And grew larger than I ever thought it would.

Those have been the moments where you've surprised me the most.

And I find myself cupping my hands and praying—
Praying for those moments to never stop coming.
When we need it most, when we don't expect it at all.
When we find ourselves apart from one another,
I hope those moments always find their way to us
In this long and joyous life.

Here's to you,
And here's to us.

May you find peace wherever you step,
May you find a cool stream wherever you settle,
And may you find unequivocal and boundless happiness
In what you set your mind to.

Peace & Blessings

Sincerely,

F.S. Yousaf

ACKNOWLEDGEMENTS

First and foremost, thank you to James for helping me achieve one of my many goals in life. I couldn't have been here without your constant support.

Thank you, Michelle, for taking a chance on me. I know how risky these things can be, but this book wouldn't be in the place it is without your support.

Nida, for igniting my inspiration to write and publish, as she once did. A person I looked up to for most of my life, and still do. Eiman, for being my rock, and a person I could wholeheartedly trust. Thank you for being someone I could turn to in times of ranting, and our (very) long talks about absolutely everything and nothing at the same time.

Imam, Osama, Shy, and Shazar for being the best friends a person can ask for. You guys supported me from the beginning and are my number one fans throughout this continuous journey, and for that you all have a steady place in my heart.

Yus—I literally wrote this whole book with you on my mind. But I'll acknowledge you anyway. You're someone who has stayed by my side no matter what I was going through or struggling with. You have been the constant in my life. One who inspires me day in and day out. Thank you for pushing me, for challenging me, and for not letting me give up on my dreams when the future looked bleak. I'll do my best to repay you one day, I promise.

And thank you to everyone who's read my work, who's sent me messages, and the ones who kept me going overall. There are so many of you, and every single word you've said to me has kept me writing. And I appreciate it, and hold those words close. I would honestly be nowhere without your consistent support.

Thank you from the bottom of my heart.